hirteen united States of America,
human events, it becomes
solve the political bands which
her, and to assume among the
and equal station to which the
entitle them, a decent respect
requires that they should
impel them to the separation.
to be self-evident,
created equal, that they are
certain unalienable Rights,
Life, Liberty and the

—A portion of The Declaration of Independence

Thomas Jefferson

Life, Liberty and the Pursuit of Everything

Maira Kalman

Nancy Paulsen Books An Imprint of Penguin Group (USA)

Thomas Jefferson

had red hair and some freckles (about 20 I think),

he grew to be very tall

and oh yes, he was **the third President of the United States.**

He was born in

1743

on a plantation

(a very large farm)

in Virginia.

What was
he interested in?

EVERYTHING.

I MEAN IT.

EVERYTHING.

He loved books. He said,

"I CANNOT LIVE WITHOUT BOOKS."

Books on history, science, philosophy, government,

mathematics, music, art and so much more.

He Read about SHREWS and SHOES and BEES and CHEESE and how to SAY PLEASE

in French,
Spanish,
Latin,
Greek,
Italian,
German and
English of course.

(He was quite polite.)

He designed and built his home
on a mountain in Virginia and called it

MONTICELLO

(which means "Little Mountain" in Italian).

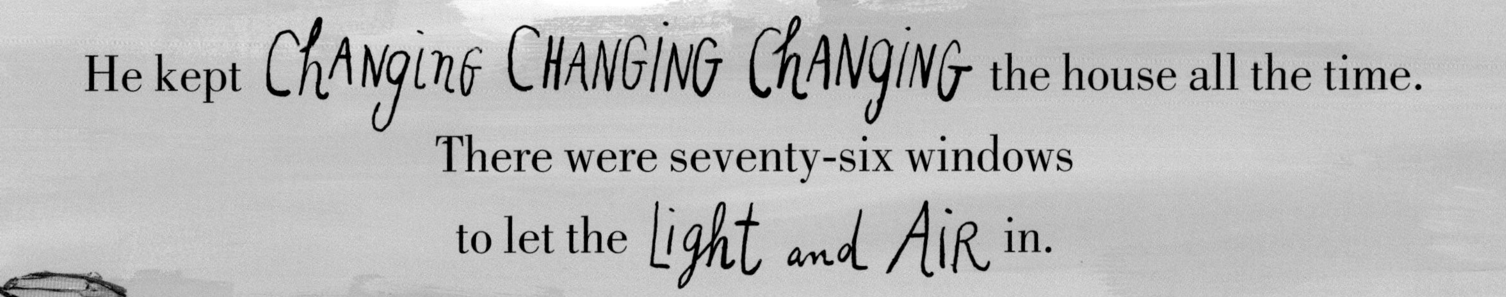

He kept CHANGING CHANGING CHANGING the house all the time.
There were seventy-six windows
to let the LIGHT and AIR in.

He loved flowers growing and fish in the pond.
Another way of saying that is he loved
FLORA and FAUNA.

The house was a MUSEUM of his MIND.

Jefferson was curious about everything. A visitor walking in would see all kinds of collections. Maps, mastodon bones, paintings, statues and Native American artifacts . . .

like this

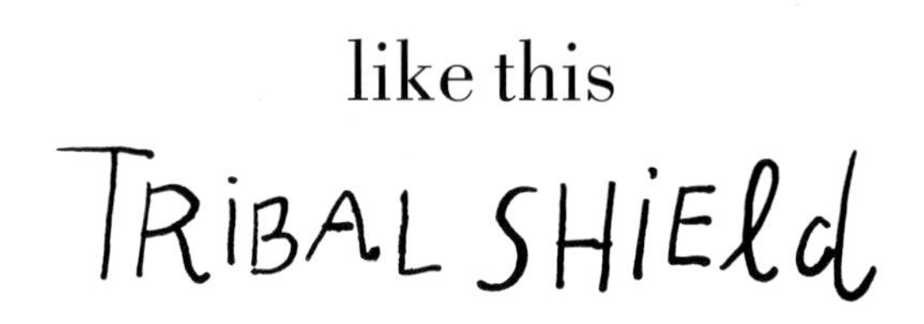

decorated with

a FIERCE and FEROCIOUS beast

that could give you nightmares.

(Ugh. Nightmares. Why do we have them?)

Even his BED was INTERESTING.

He designed it to be open to two different rooms. Jefferson slept slightly sitting up so he was ready to spring out of bed at the first light of dawn. He wanted to DO things. He could either go into his study with his ingenious copying machine and rotating book stand, OR he could get OUT of BED on the OTHER SIDE, jump INTO his BOOTS and GO OUTSIDE.

Often he would go to his

VEGETABLE GARDEN.

Thomas Jefferson loved his garden almost more than anything.

He believed people should take care of the land

and grow healthy food.

A GARDEN makes PEOPLE HAPPY.

He thought vegetables
should be the main course
and meat a side dish.

His favorite vegetable was
PEAS.
PEAS REALLY ARE WONDERFUL
and FUN TO COUNT.

Pea List

Arkansas
Black-eyed
Cowpea
Everlasting
Hotspur
Marrowfat
Pearl
Prince Albert
Prussian Blue
(and more)

He also Loved

MUSIC.

He practiced his violin

three hours a day.

HOW

did he

have TIME

for THAT?

He had a GOOD LIFE, full of WORK and LOVE.

But sadly, his beloved wife, Martha, died young.

Four of their six children died before they reached adulthood.

Here is his DARLING PATSY,

the only child that lived longer than he did.

Jefferson wanted her to be a smart woman

and gave her this advice:

"Determine Never to be Idle.
No person will have occasion to Complain
of the want of Time who never Loses Any."

That means

"DON'T BE LAZY."

(It is boring to be Lazy.)

But wait.

We have not spoken of

the Founding of America.

There were many people
who wanted the colonies
to be free of the tyrannical
rule of the English king.
They all wanted freedom and
were prepared to fight for it.

The brilliant Benjamin Franklin
of the CRAZY GREAT HAT
was one of them.

So was John Adams,
of the Fiery Temper.
He and Jefferson
were close friends
EXCEPT
when they were Fighting.

And of course there was George Washington, another tall redhead (but who could know under that powdered wig?).
He would command the army during the Revolutionary War.
He wore a set of

FALSE TEETH

made from

IVORY and WIRES.

They fit him BADLY and HURT him SO.

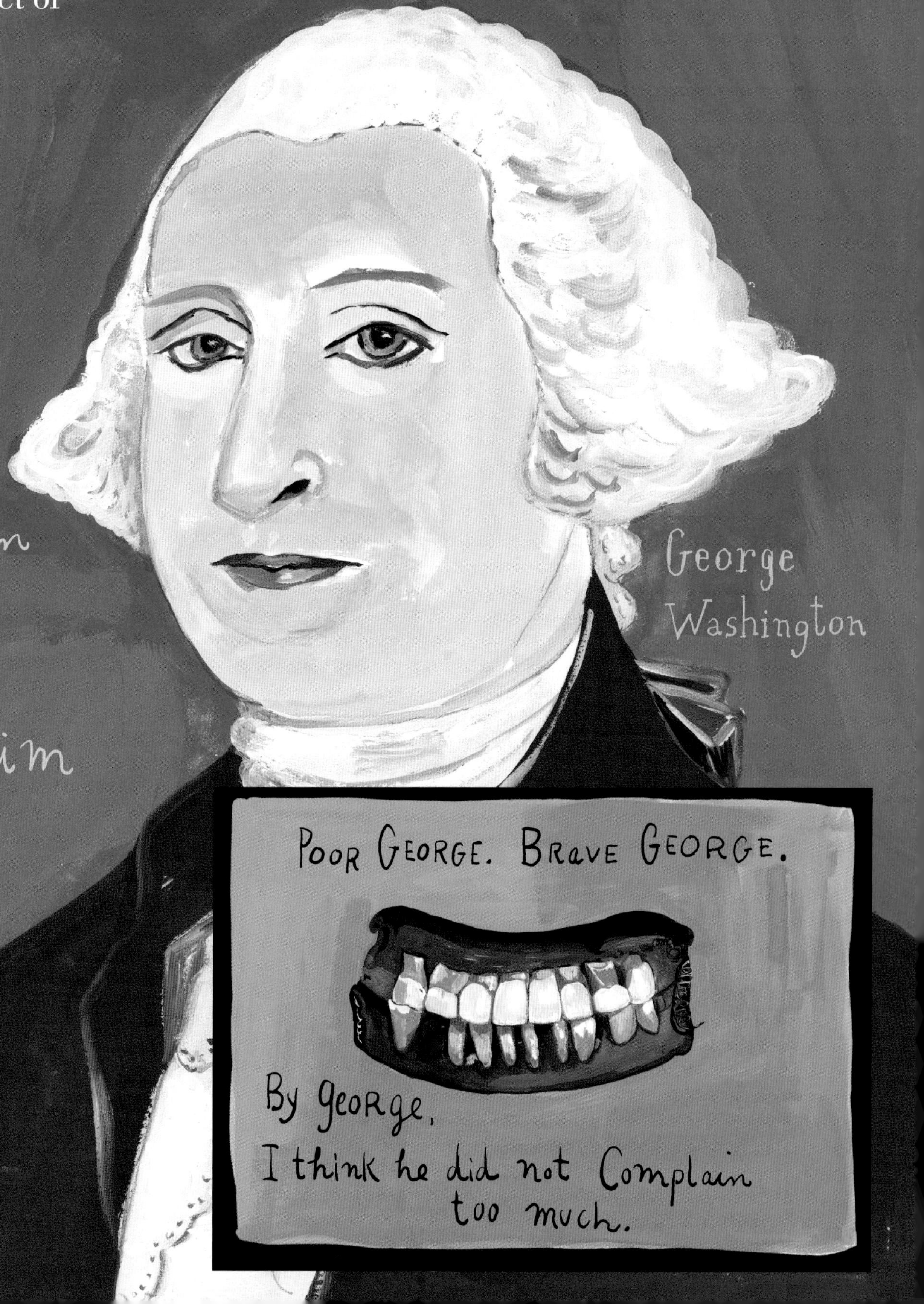

George Washington

Poor George. Brave George.

By George, I think he did not complain too much.

Many men met in this room in Philadelphia to debate the future.
Thomas Jefferson, who was a terrible speaker but a great writer,
was chosen to write

the DECLARATION of INDEPENDENCE.

It is one of the greatest documents ever written and
a beacon of liberty for people all over the world:

We hold these truths to be self-evident, that all men are created equal, that they are endowed by their Creator with certain unalienable Rights, that among these are Life, Liberty and the Pursuit of Happiness.

It would be many years until most Americans were treated equally
but it was the ideal on which America was founded
and it is still strived for today.

The AMERICAN REVOLUTION was fought and the colonies
were now independent of Britain. George Washington was
elected first president of the United States of America.
John Adams was elected the second president.

And in 1800,

Thomas Jefferson

was elected third President of the United States.

He was a strong leader with many ideas.
He believed in separation of church and state.
That means that all people should be free to practice whatever religion they like.
Religion should not be part of government.

PRESIDENT JEFFERSON bought LAND from NAPOLEON,

RED Haired William Clark

This PART is the Louisiana Purchase of 1803

Flora

NATIVE AMERICAN ARTIFACTS

the brilliant and fierce emperor of France,

and doubled the size of the United States.

(Napoleon needed money.)

It was called

THE LOUISIANA PURCHASE.

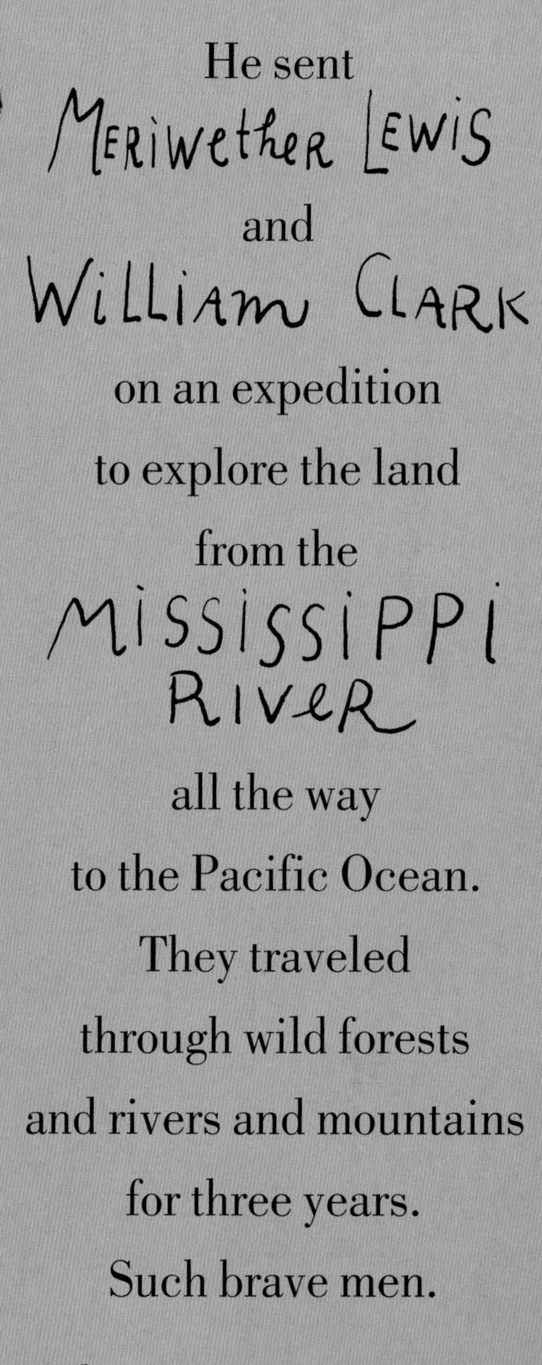

He sent
MERIWETHER LEWIS
and
WILLIAM CLARK
on an expedition
to explore the land
from the
MISSISSIPPI
RIVER
all the way
to the Pacific Ocean.
They traveled
through wild forests
and rivers and mountains
for three years.
Such brave men.

They met many Native
American tribespeople,
including
SACAGAWEA.
She was only a teenager,
but she helped guide them.

When Jefferson completed his presidency, he went back to his beloved Monticello. His friend the MARQUIS de LAFAYETTE, a Frenchman who helped in the revolution, came to visit.

They would STROLL through the gardens PLUCKING FIGS from the TREES.

And while they ate the delicious figs, they would pass the slave quarters on Mulberry Row. The man who said of slavery

"This ABOMINATION MUST END"

was the OWNER OF ABOUT 150 SLAVES.

The MONUMENTAL MAN had MONUMENTAL FLAWS.

The slaves lived in cramped rooms with few possessions.

What did they do? EVERYTHING. They toiled and cooked and labored in the fields from dawn to dusk.

Jefferson would visit the kitchen each week and wind the grandfather clock.

He PROBABLY SAID a FEW Kind WORds to the COOKS.

In the FANCY DINING ROOM they had the BEST of EVERYTHING.

Even Vanilla ice cream! And so many kinds of pudding—apple, bread, huckleberry, lemon, macaroni, orange, plum, quince and tapioca pudding, all produced by the endless labor of slaves. Jefferson may have been a kind master, but it was still a horror.

Here is Jefferson's farm book
with a list of his slaves and
the supplies they were given.

OUR hearts are BROKEN.

136 1810. Dec.	linen	pl.[na]	cottn	blankt	bed	hat	sifh
Burwell							
Edwin	7	$5\frac{1}{2}$				1.	
Joe	7	$5\frac{1}{2}$				1.	
Edy	homespun						
James 05							
Maria 07							
Davy	7	3	$2\frac{1}{2}$			1.	
Fanny							
Ellen 09							
Amy							
Critta							
Sally							
Beverly 98	$4\frac{2}{3}$	2	$1\frac{3}{4}$				
Harriet 01							
Madison 05							
Eston 08							
Betty Brown				1			
Robert 99							
Mary 01							
Peter Hemings	7	3	$2\frac{1}{2}$	1			
Nance				1			1

One of the names is SALLY.

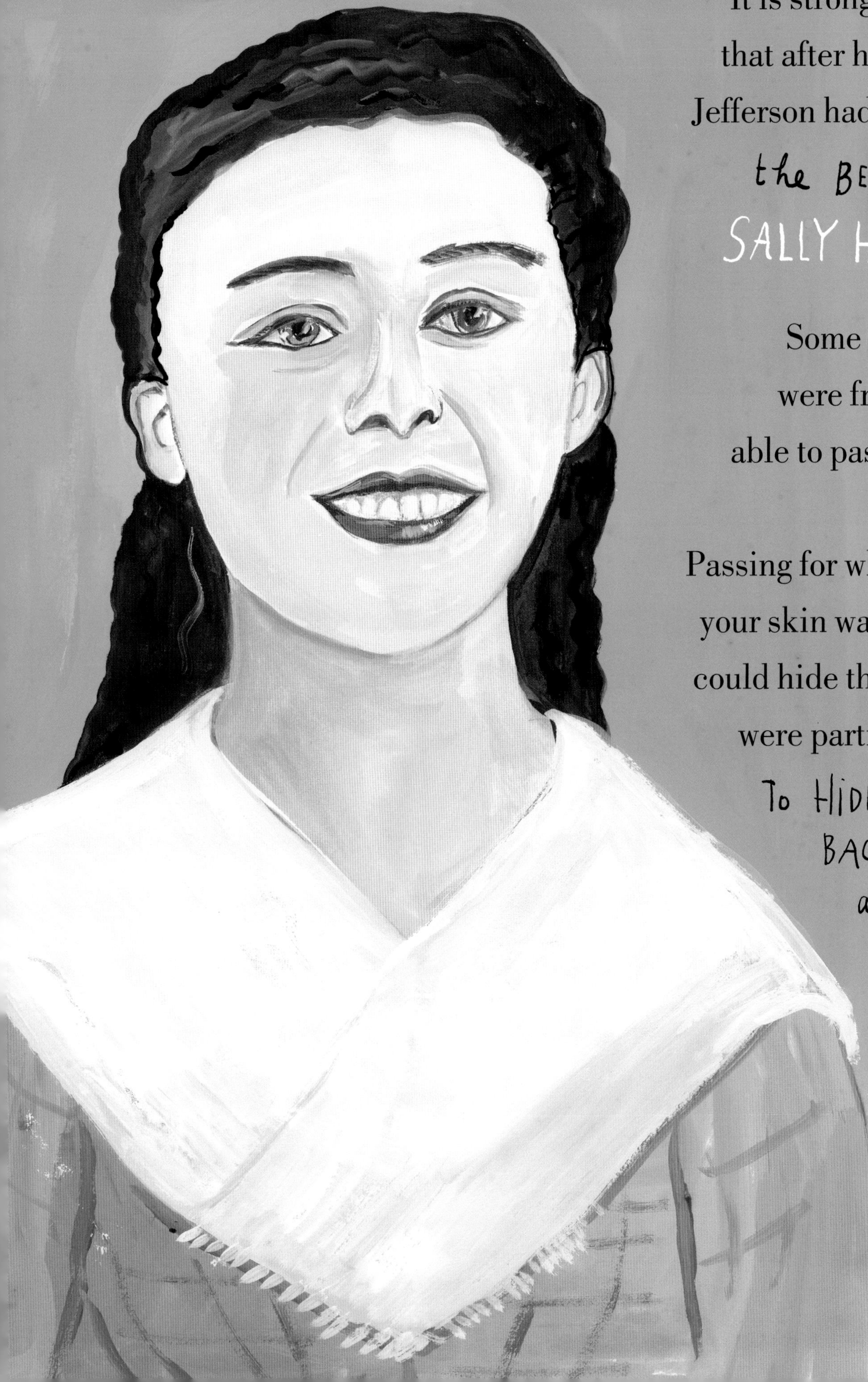

It is strongly believed
that after his wife died,
Jefferson had children with
the BEAUTIFUL
SALLY HEMINGS.

Some of them
were freed and
able to pass for white.

Passing for white meant that
your skin was so light, you
could hide the fact that you
were partially black.
To HIDE your
BACKGROUND is
a VERY SAD
THING.
Perhaps People
FELT They had
NO CHOICE
in such a
PREJUDICED
LAND.

As Jefferson got older, he spent more time outdoors.
He no longer cared for FANCY CLOTHES.

His torn jacket was repaired with SOCKS.

He carried a penknife with many tools,
and would spend many hours riding his horse or walking
through his garden and land.

He wrote to his friend,
"The OBJECT of WALKING is to RELAX the Mind.
You should therefore not permit yourself even to THINK
while you walk, but divert yourself by the objects surrounding you.
WALKING IS THE
BEST
POSSIBLE
EXERCISE."

He also had good advice
about being mad.
"When you are ANGRY,
count TEN BEFORE
you SPEAK;
if VERY ANGRY, to 100."

He still read many books (his books were the beginning of the Library of Congress) and founded a university. There was always much to be done.

On July 4th 1826 at the Age of 83 this Extraordinary man Died.

The same day as his friend John Adams.

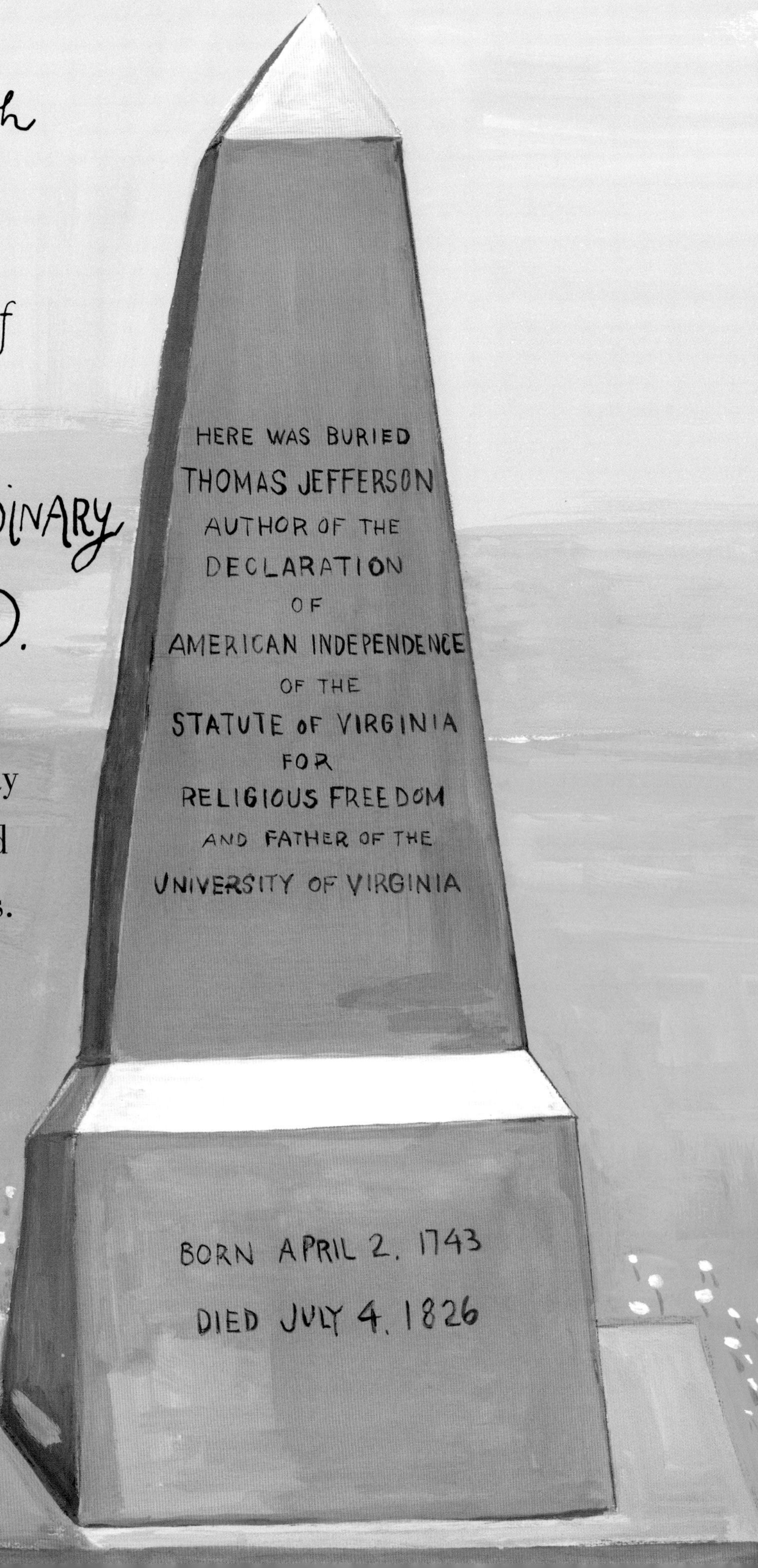

HERE WAS BURIED
THOMAS JEFFERSON
AUTHOR OF THE
DECLARATION
OF
AMERICAN INDEPENDENCE
OF THE
STATUTE OF VIRGINIA
FOR
RELIGIOUS FREEDOM
AND FATHER OF THE
UNIVERSITY OF VIRGINIA

BORN APRIL 2. 1743
DIED JULY 4. 1826

He is Buried at Monticello

under the gravestone

that he designed.

He wrote his own Epitaph

and he did not mention

being president.

(I wonder why.)

If you want to understand
this country and its people
and what it means to be OPTIMISTIC
and COMPLEX and Tragic and Wrong and
Courageous, You Need to go to Monticello.

Walk around the house and the gardens.
The linden trees might be in bloom,
filling the air with their delicious perfume.
Maybe you will lie down under a tree
and fall asleep thinking about
LIFE, LIBERTY and the PURSUIT of EVERYTHING.

Notes

Monticello

Monticello (pronounced "mon-tih-CHEL-oh") is the plantation in Virginia that Thomas Jefferson designed and called home for most of his life. Jefferson referred to Monticello as his "essay on architecture" and he continued to work on it for more than forty years. It is now a U.S. National Historic Landmark and UNESCO World Heritage Site that visitors can tour year round. Its image is featured on the U.S. nickel.

Jefferson's Library

Jefferson sold his library of books by the world's greatest writers, philosophers and scientists to the Library of Congress to help replace the books lost when the U.S. Capitol was burnt by the British during the War of 1812.

Vegetable Garden

Jefferson was an avid gardener who experimented with growing hundreds of plant varieties from around the world in his thousand-foot-long garden, including Italian broccoli, French figs, Mexican peppers, and beans collected on the Lewis and Clark expedition.

Jefferson's Wife

Martha Wayles Skelton Jefferson (1748–1782) was a widow of twenty-three when she married Thomas Jefferson. Only two of their six children survived to adulthood. Martha died years before her husband became president. Jefferson was devastated by her loss and was said to have sworn to her on her deathbed he would not remarry.

Jefferson's Daughter

Martha Jefferson Randolph (1772–1836), known as "Patsy," was the eldest and longest-surviving daughter of Thomas and Martha Jefferson. She and her husband, Thomas Mann Randolph Jr., had twelve children; eleven survived to adulthood.

British King

Many colonists—British American citizens—remained loyal to King George III even into the spring of 1776. But his unwillingness to compromise and listen to their complaints made them realize independence was the only solution.

Revolutionary War

Great Britain's thirteen North American colonies won autonomy from the British crown in what was also known as the U.S. War of Independence, lasting from 1775 to 1783.

Founding Fathers

America's "Founding Fathers" are the political leaders who led the American Revolution and the founding of the new independent nation. They devised a new government based on the revolutionary idea that ordinary people could govern themselves.

Declaration of Independence

The Second Continental Congress appointed a committee of five men to write a Declaration of Independence from British rule. Jefferson wrote the first draft, setting forth the ideals of the new nation and the reasons for separating from British rule. Church bells rang out in Philadelphia on July 4, 1776, the day the Declaration of Independence was adopted and our nation was officially born.

Benjamin Franklin

Benjamin Franklin worked with Thomas Jefferson on the final draft of the Declaration of Independence. As a diplomat in Paris, Franklin was famous for his literary and scientific achievements and for wearing his coonskin hat that made him look like a rugged American frontiersman. Jefferson thought Franklin was one of the greatest men of the age.

John Adams

John Adams and Thomas Jefferson were fellow patriots who became political rivals when they disagreed about how the country should be governed. Adams, a Federalist, ran against Jefferson, a Democratic-Republican, to become the second president of the United States; later, Jefferson beat Adams to become the third. They renewed their friendship years later and corresponded regularly until their deaths—both dying on July 4, 1826, fifty years after the Declaration was adopted.

George Washington

The Second Continental Congress voted to form the Continental Army to fight the British, and George Washington was chosen as its commander-in-chief. He became the first U.S. president in 1789. Throughout his life, Washington suffered from poor dental health and had numerous sets of dentures made from ivory, gold, and human and animal teeth.

Separation of Church and State

Jefferson believed religion was a personal matter. In 1779, he introduced a Bill for Establishing Religious Freedom in Virginia that prohibited the government from either regulating or endorsing specific religions.

Louisiana Purchase

President Jefferson doubled the size of the United States in 1803 and secured the port of New Orleans when he purchased the Louisiana Territory from France for $15 million—about four cents per acre—and opened up the continent to its westward expansion.

Lewis and Clark Expedition

Jefferson's dream of exploring the Northwest Territory came true in May 1804 when he sent out the Lewis and Clark expedition to explore the uncharted west, observe the Native American tribes and study the plants, animals, geology and terrain of the region. He also hoped to find routes to the Pacific Ocean.

Sacagawea

As a child, Sacagawea was kidnapped and sold to a French Canadian fur trader named Toussaint Charbonneau, who later married her. When they joined the Lewis and Clark expedition, they had their two-month-old son in tow. The sole woman on the journey, she served as a translator and guide.

Marquis de Lafayette

When Marie Joseph Paul Yves Roche Gilbert du Motier, Marquis de Lafayette, was nineteen years old, he sailed from France to America to aid the colonists in the Revolutionary War, knowing only the English he'd learned during his 54-day voyage. He was known for his skill and courage in battle.

Mulberry Row

This 1,300-foot-long road lined with mulberry trees was the center of Monticello's plantation activity. Its over twenty structures included a blacksmith shop, carpenter shop, textile factory, smokehouse, dairy, storehouses, stable, and dwellings for both free and enslaved workers.

Jefferson's Slaves

The Monticello slaves worked from dawn to dusk every day but Sundays and holidays to keep Monticello running. Those under age ten helped care for younger children or did light tasks. From ages ten to fifteen, their work included making nails and spinning cloth. At sixteen, they were considered adults, shifting to farm labor or learning trades.

Sally Hemings

Jefferson inherited Sally Hemings from his father-in-law. She was his daughters' maid, and later a seamstress and household servant. Some controversy remains about whether or not Jefferson was the father of her six children—he never commented on it publicly.

University of Virginia

Thomas Jefferson founded the University of Virginia in 1819 and it was the first state university to be established without any connections to a church. He wrote that it would be dedicated to "the illimitable freedom of the human mind."

Special thanks to the Thomas Jefferson Foundation,
who maintain and run Monticello—
for more information, go to www.monticello.org.

for lulu and alexander kalman
who inspire my life at every turn

thank you
to my editor nancy paulsen
the art and design team cecilia yung and marikka tamura
at penguin books
for wise and beautiful leadership and assistance.
thank you to my agent charlotte sheedy a force of nature. a force for good.
and to susan stein, curator/vp at Thomas Jefferson's Monticello,
who invited me to monticello in the first place (a dream come true)
with intelligence and thoughtfulness
offering me an unparalleled view of a life-changing place.
who could ask for anything more?

NANCY PAULSEN BOOKS
Published by the Penguin Group
Penguin Group (USA) LLC
375 Hudson Street, New York, NY 10014

USA | Canada | UK | Ireland | Australia
New Zealand | India | South Africa | China
penguin.com
A Penguin Random House Company

Library of Congress Cataloging-in-Publication Data is available upon request.

Manufactured in China by South China Printing Co. Ltd.
ISBN 978-0-399-24040-9
1 3 5 7 9 10 8 6 4 2

Design by Marikka Tamura.
Text set in Bodoni Std. The art was done in gouache.

IN CONGRESS, July 4, 1776.

The unanim eclaration of the

When ourse of

necessary fo le to d

have conne and

powers of th ra

Laws of Nature a s Go

to the opinions o kind

declare the causes whic

We hold these truth

that all men are

endowed by their Creator wi

that among these are

pursuit of Happiness